Hymns for Occasions
for Manuals

Hymns for Occasions
for Manuals

One hundred special arrangements

Colin Mawby

Kevin Mayhew

We hope you enjoy the music in this book. Further copies are available
from your local music shop or Christian bookshop.

In case of difficulty, please contact the publisher direct by writing to:

The Sales Department
KEVIN MAYHEW LTD
Rattlesden
Bury St Edmunds
Suffolk
IP30 0SZ

Phone 01449 737978
Fax 01449 737834

Please ask for our complete catalogue of outstanding Church Music.

Also available: *Hymns for Occasions*   1400026
                    More Hymns for Occasions   1400112

First published in Great Britain in 1997 by Kevin Mayhew Ltd.

ISBN 0 84003 066 6
ISMN M 57004 097 1
Catalogue No: 1400153

0 1 2 3 4 5 6 7 8 9

Front Cover: *Music-making Angel* by Melezzo da Forli.
Courtesy of SuperStock Ltd., London. Reproduced by kind permission.

Cover design by Jaquetta Sergeant

Music Editors: Donald Thomson and Rosalind Welch
Music setting by Tracy Cracknell and Daniel Kelly

Printed and bound in Great Britain by
Caligraving Limited Thetford Norfolk

Contents

Foreword

The arrangements in *Hymns for Occasions for Manuals* are intended for use at those times when the organist is looking for extra material to add interest and splendour to the hymn singing.

All the arrangements include an introduction, the standard harmonisation of the hymn tune, a passage which leads into a more complex last verse harmonisation, and a concluding few bars. The introduction (which always contains enough of the hymn tune to act as an encouragement to the congregation) should normally be used only before the first verse of the hymn, and subsequent verses should all end with the passage marked with a first-time bar. In the penultimate verse the organist should follow the directions marked in the second-time bar, proceeding via the linking passage into the last verse arrangement. The conclusion provides a flourish. Both the introduction and the conclusion are optional – the organist should choose to use all or part of each arrangement as befitting the occasion.

I hope *Hymns for Occasions for Manuals* will provide yet more useful music for parish organists at a time when hymn singing is already enjoying a remarkable renaissance.

COLIN MAWBY

1 ADESTE FIDELES

Metre: Irregular
Melody: John Francis Wade (1711-1786)

2 ALL FOR JESUS

2. Lead into last verse

Last verse

Conclusion

Metre: 87 87
Melody: John Stainer (1840-1901)

3 ALL THINGS BRIGHT AND BEAUTIFUL

Metre: 76 76 and Refrain
Melody: William Henry Monk (1823-1889)

4 ANGEL VOICES

Last verse

Conclusion

Metre: 85 85 843
Melody: Edwin George Monk (1819-1900)

5 ANIMA CHRISTI

16

Metre: 10 10 10 10
Melody: William Maher (1823-1877)

6 AR HYD Y NOS

Last verse

Conclusion

Metre: 84 84 88 84
Melody: Traditional Welsh

19

7 AURELIA

2. Lead into last verse

Last verse

Conclusion

Metre: 76 76 D
Melody: Samuel Sebastian Wesley (1810-1876)

21

8 AUSTRIA

Metre: 87 87 D
Melody: Croation folk tune adapted by Franz Joseph Haydn (1732-1809)

9 BATTLE HYMN

Refrain

1. D.S. for more verses

Refrain

Conclusion

Metre: 14 15 15 6 and Refrain
Melody: Traditional American

10 BELMONT

Metre: 86 86 (CM)
Melody: Adapted from William Gardiner's 'Sacred Melodies' (1815)

11 BILLING

Metre: 86 86 (CM)
Melody: Richard Runciman Terry (1865-1938)

12 BLAENWERN

Last verse

Conclusion

Metre: 87 87 D
Melody: William Rowlands (1860-1937)

13 BROTHER JAMES'S AIR

Metre: 86 86 (CM)
Melody: Brother Leith MacBeth Bain (c.1860 - 1925)

14 BUCKLAND

2. Lead into last verse

Last verse

Conclusion

Metre: 77 77
Melody: Leighton George Hayne (1836-1883)

15 BUNESSAN

Introduction

Verses

1. D.S. for more verses | **2. Lead into last verse**

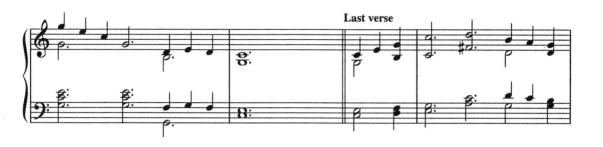

Last verse

Conclusion

Metre: 55 54 D
Melody: Traditional Gaelic

16 CARLISLE

42

Last verse

Conclusion

Metre: 66 86 (SM)
Melody: Charles Lockhart (1745-1815)

17 CASWALL

Metre: 65 65
Melody: Friedrich Filitz (1804-1876)

18 CHORUS ANGELORUM

Metre: 86 86 C
Melody: Arthur Somervell (1863-1937)

19 CRADLE SONG

Metre: 11 11 11 11
Melody: William James Kirkpatrick (1838-1921)

20 CRANHAM

Metre: Irregular
Melody and harmony for verses: Gustav Holst (1874-1934)

51

21 CRIMOND

Metre: 86 86 (CM)
Melody: Jessie Seymour Irvine (1836-1887)

22 CRÜGER

Metre: 76 76 D
Melody: Johann Crüger (1598-1662) adapted by William Henry Monk (1823-1889)

23 CULBACH

Last verse

Conclusion

Metre: 77 77
Melody: Adapted from Johann Scheiffler's 'Heilige Seelenlust' (1657)

24 CWM RHONDDA

Metre: 87 87 47
Melody: John Hughes (1873-1932)

25 DARWALL'S 148th

2. Lead into last verse

Last verse

Conclusion

Metre: 66 66 44 44
Melody: John Darwall (1731-1789)

26 DIADEMATA

Introduction

Verses

1. D.S. for more verses

Metre: 66 86 D (DSM)
Melody: George Job Elvey (1816-1893)

27 DIX

Introduction

𝄋 Verses

1. D.S. for more verses

2. Lead into last verse

Last verse

Conclusion

Metre: 77 77 77
Melody: Conrad Kocher (1786-1872)

65

28 DOMINUS REGIT ME

2. Lead into last verse

Last verse

Conclusion

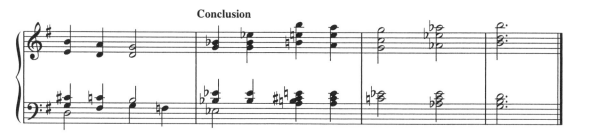

Metre: 87 87
Melody: John Bacchus Dykes (1823-1876)

29 EASTER HYMN

Last verse

Conclusion

Metre: 77 77 and Alleluias
Melody: From 'Lyra Davidica' (1708)

69

30 ELLACOMBE

70

Metre: 76 76 D
Melody: from 'Württemberg Gesangbuch' (1784)

31 EVELYNS

72

Last verse

Conclusion

Metre: 65 65 D
Melody: William Henry Monk (1823-1889)

32 EVENTIDE

Introduction

Verses

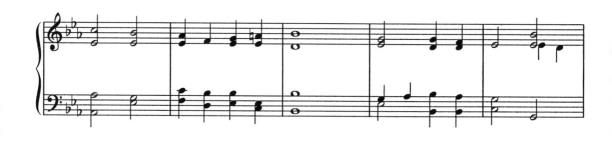

1. D.S. for more verses

Metre: 10 10 10 10
Melody: William Henry Monk (1823-1889)

33 EWING

Metre: 76 76 D
Melody: Alexander Ewing (1830-1895)

34 FULDA

Metre: 88 88 (LM)
Melody: From William Gardiner's 'Sacred Melodies' (1815)

79

35 GERONTIUS

Last verse

Conclusion

Metre: 86 86 (CM)
Melody: John Bacchus Dykes (1823-1876)

36 GOPSAL

Metre: 66 66 88
Melody: George Frideric Handel (1685-1759)

37 GWALCHMAI

2. **Lead into last verse**   *molto rit.*

Last verse
a tempo

Conclusion

Metre: 74 74 D
Melody: Joseph David Jones (1827-1870)

85

38 HANOVER

Metre: 10 10 11 11
Melody: William Croft (1678-1727)

39 HELMSLEY

1. D.S. for more verses

2. Lead into last verse

Last verse

Conclusion

Metre: 87 87 47
Melody: From John Wesley's 'Select Hymns' (1765)

90

40 HIGHWOOD

Metre: 11 10 11 10

Melody and harmony for verses: Richard Runciman Terry (1865-1938)

41 HORSLEY

94

2. Lead into last verse

Last verse

Conclusion

Metre: 86 86 (CM)
Melody: William Horsley (1774-1858)

42 HYFRYDOL

1. D.S. for more verses

2. Lead into last verse

Last verse

Conclusion

Metre: 87 87 D
Melody: Rowland Huw Pritchard (1811-1887)

43 IRBY

Last verse
a tempo

Conclusion

Metre: 87 87 77
Melody: Henry John Gauntlett (1805-1876)

44 LASST UNS ERFREUEN

2. Lead into last verse

Tuba

Last verse

Conclusion

Metre: 88 44 88 and Alleluias
Melody: From 'Geistliche Kirchengesang', Cologne (1623)

45 LAUDATE DOMINUM

Metre: 10 10 11 11
Melody: Hubert Parry (1848-1918)

46 LAUS DEO (Redhead No. 46)

Last verse

Conclusion

Metre: 87 87
Melody: Richard Redhead (1820-1901)

47 LEONI

2. Lead into last verse

Last verse

Conclusion

Metre: 66 84 D
Melody: Traditional Hebrew

48 LLANFAIR

Metre: 77 77 and Alleluias

Melody: Robert Williams (1781-1821)

49 LOBE DEN HERREN

Introduction

𝄋 Verses

1. D.S. for more verses

2. Lead into last verse

Last verse

Conclusion

Metre: 14 14 4 7 8
Melody: From 'Praxis Pietatis Melica' (1668)

50 LOVE DIVINE

Last verse
a tempo

Conclusion

Metre: 87 87
Melody: John Stainer (1840-1901)

51 MACCABAEUS

Metre: 10 11 11 11 and Refrain
Melody: George Frideric Handel (1685-1759)

52 MANNHEIM

Last verse

Conclusion

Metre: 87 87 87
Melody: Friedrich Filitz (1804-1876)

53 MELCOMBE

2. Lead into last verse

Last verse

Conclusion

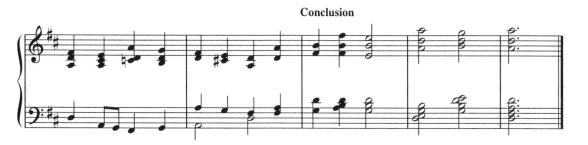

Metre: 88 88 (LM)
Melody: Samuel Webbe (1740-1816)

54 MELITA

Introduction

§ Verses

1. D.S. for more verses

2. Lead into last verse

Last verse

Conclusion

Metre: 88 88 88
Melody: John Bacchus Dykes (1823-1876)

125

55 MENDELSSOHN

126

2. **Lead into last verse**

Last verse

Refrain

Conclusion

Metre: 77 77 D 77
Melody: Felix Mendelssohn (1809-1847)

56 MILES LANE

Introduction

Last verse

Conclusion

Metre: 86 86 (CM)
Melody: William Shrubsole (1760-1806)

129

57 MONKLAND

Introduction

Verses

Refrain

1. D.S. for more verses

2. Lead into last verse

Last verse

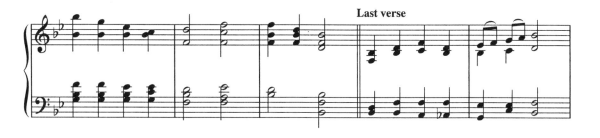

Refrain

Conclusion

Metre: 77 77
Melody: John Antes (1740-1811)

58 MOSCOW

Metre: 664 66 64
Melody: Felice de Giardini (1716-1796)

59 NARENZA

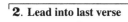

2. **Lead into last verse**

Last verse

Conclusion

Metre: 66 86 (SM)
Melody: From Leisentritt's 'Catholicum Hymnologium Germanicum' (1584)
adapted by William Henry Havergal (1793-1870)

60 NICAEA

2. Lead into last verse

Last verse

Conclusion

Metre: 11 12 12 10
Melody: John Bacchus Dykes (1823-1876)

61 NOEL NOUVELET

138

2. Lead into last verse

Last verse

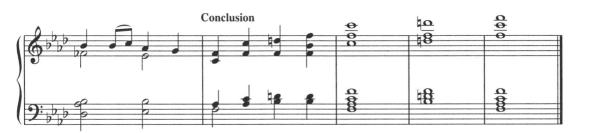

Conclusion

Metre: 11 11 10 11
Melody: Traditional French

62 NUN DANKET

2. Lead into last verse

Last verse

Conclusion

Metre: 67 67 66 66
Melody: Johann Crüger (1598-1662)

63 OLD HUNDREDTH

Introduction
Tuba

𝄋 Verses

1. D.S. for more verses

2. Lead into last verse

Last verse

Conclusion

Metre: 88 88 (LM)
Melody: From the 'Genevan Psalter' (1551)

64 PADERBORN

Introduction

Verses

1. D.S. for more verses | 2. Lead into last verse

Last verse

Conclusion

Metre: 10 10 11 11
Melody: From 'Paderborn Gesangbuch' (1765)

145

65 PASSION CHORALE

Metre: 76 76 D
Melody: Hans Leo Hassler (1564-1612)

66 PERSONENT HODIE

Last verse

Refrain

Conclusion

Metre: 666 66 and Refrain
Melody: From 'Piae Cantiones' (1582)

67 PICARDY

Last verse

Conclusion

Metre: 87 87 87
Melody: Traditional French carol

68 PRAISE MY SOUL

152

Last verse

Conclusion

Metre: 87 87 87
Melody: John Goss (1800-1880)

153

69 REGENT SQUARE

154

Metre: 87 87 87
Melody: Henry Smart (1813-1879)

70 REPTON

156

2. Lead into last verse

Last verse

Conclusion

Metre: 86 88 6
Melody: Hubert Parry (1848-1918)

71 RICHMOND

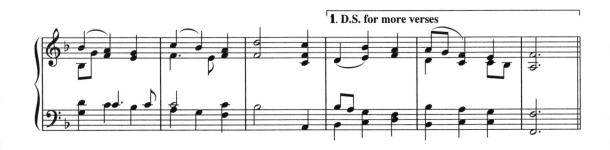

Metre: 86 86 (CM)
Melody: Thomas Haweis (1734-1820)

72 ROCKINGHAM

Metre: 88.88 (LM)
Melody: Adapted by Edward Miller (1735-1807)

73 ROYAL OAK

2. Lead into last verse

Last verse

Refrain

Conclusion

Metre: 76 76 and Refrain
Melody: Traditional English

74 SAFFRON WALDEN

Metre: 88 86
Melody: Arthur Henry Brown (1830-1926)

75 ST BERNARD

Last verse

Conclusion

Metre: 86 86 (CM)
Melody: Adapted from 'Tochter Sion' (1741)

76 ST CLEMENT

Metre: 98 98
Melody: Clement Cotterill Scholefield (1839-1904)

77 ST COLUMBA

Metre: 87 87
Melody: Traditional Irish

78 ST DENIO

Last verse

Conclusion

Metre: 11 11 11 11
Melody: Traditional Welsh from John Roberts' 'Caniadau y Cyssegre' (1839)

79 ST FULBERT

Introduction

𝄋 Verses

1. D.S. for
more verses

2. Lead into last verse

Last verse

Conclusion

Metre: 86 86 (CM)
Melody: Henry John Gauntlett (1805-1876)

80 ST THEODULPH

Metre: 76 76 D
Melody: Melchior Teschner (1584-1635)

81 ST THOMAS (Webbe)

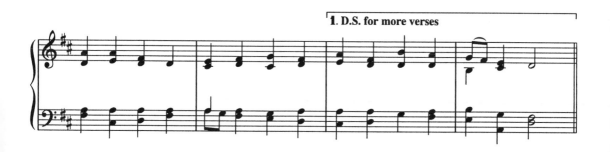

Metre: 87 87 87
Melody: Samuel Webbe (1740-1816)

82 ST THOMAS (Williams)

Last verse

Conclusion

Metre: 66 86 (SM)
Melody: Aaron Williams (1731-1776)

83 SALZBURG

Metre: 77 77 D
Melody: Jacob Hintze (1622-1702)

84 SANDYS

Metre: 66 86 (SM)
Melody: From William Sandys' 'Christmas Carols' (1833)

85 SING HOSANNA

Metre: 10 8 10 9 and Refrain
Melody: Traditional

86 SLANE

Metre: 10 11 11 11
Melody: Traditional Irish

87 SONG 34 (Angels' Song)

190

Metre: 88 88 (LM)
Melody: Orlando Gibbons (1583-1625)

88 STILLE NACHT

2. Lead into last verse

Last verse

Conclusion

Metre: Irregular
Melody: Franz Grüber (1787-1863)

89 STRENGTH AND STAY

194

Metre: 11 10 11 10
Melody: John Bacchus Dykes (1823-1876)

90 STUTTGART

Metre: 87 87
Melody: Christian Friedrich Witt (1660-1716)

91 SURREY

Metre: 88 88 88
Melody: Henry Carey (c.1690-1743)

92 TALLIS'S CANON

2. Lead into last verse

Last verse

Conclusion

Metre: 88 88 (LM)
Melody: Thomas Tallis (c.1505-1585)

93 TALLIS'S ORDINAL

Introduction

𝄋 Verses

1. D.S. for more verses

2. Lead into last verse

Last verse

Conclusion

Metre: 86 86 (CM)
Melody: Thomas Tallis (c.1505-1585)

94 THE FIRST NOWELL

Refrain

1. D.S. for more verses   **2**. Lead into last verse

Last verse

Refrain

Conclusion

Metre: Irregular
Melody: Traditional English carol

95 THIS JOYFUL EASTERTIDE

1. D.S. for more verses   **2.** Lead into last verse

Tuba

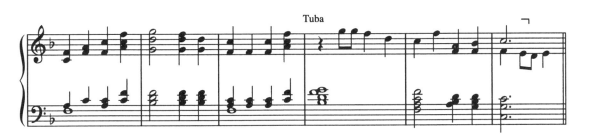

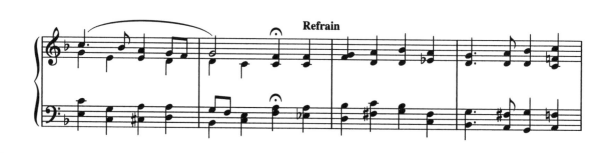

Conclusion
Tuba

Metre: 67 67 and Refrain
Melody: From 'David's Psalmen', Amsterdam (1685)

96 WAREHAM

Metre: 88 88 (LM)
Melody: William Knapp (1698-1768)

97 WAS LEBET

Metre: 13 10 13 10
Melody: From 'Rheinhardt MS' (1754)

98 WESTMINSTER ABBEY

Metre: 87 87 87
Melody: Henry Purcell (1659-1695)

99 WINCHESTER NEW

Last verse

Conclusion

Metre: 88 88 (LM)
Melody: 'Musikalisches Hand-Buch' (1690)

100 WIR PFLÜGEN

2. Lead into last verse

Last verse

Refrain

Conclusion

Metre: 76 76 D and Refrain
Melody: Johann Abraham Peter Schulz (1747-1800)

221

Metrical Index